RODGERS AND HAMMERSTEIN™

UKULELE

THE SOUND OF MUSIC

ISBN 978-1-4950-9821-5

WILLIAMSON MUSIC®

EXCLUSIVELY DISTRIBUTED BY

HAL•LEONARD®

7777 W. BLUEMOUND RD. P.O. BOX 13819 MILWAUKEE, WI 53213

In Australia Contact:
Hal Leonard Australia Pty. Ltd
4 Lentara Court
Cheltenham, Victoria, 3192 Australia
Email: ausadmin@halleonard.com.au

Visit Hal Leonard Online at
www.halleonard.com

Climb Ev'ry Mountain

Lyrics by Oscar Hammerstein II
Music by Richard Rodgers

Edelweiss

Lyrics by Oscar Hammerstein II
Music by Richard Rodgers

Bridge

Blos - som of snow, may you bloom and

grow, bloom and grow for -

Chorus

ev - er. E - del - weiss,

e - del - weiss, bless my

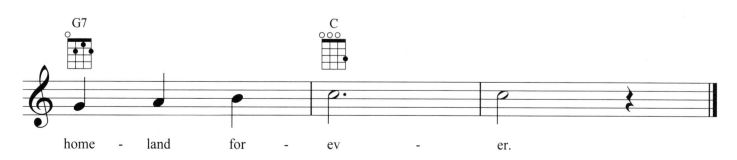

home - land for - ev - er.

I Have Confidence

Lyrics and Music by Richard Rodgers

nights of peace - ful slum - bers. When you wake up, wake up! __
chil - dren, heav - en bless them, They will look up to me __

Outro-Verse

N.C.   C   G7

___ It's health - y. All I trust I leave my heart to. ___
___ and mind me. With each step I am more cer - tain. ___

C   G7

___ All I trust be - comes my own. ___
___ Ev - 'ry - thing will turn out fine. ___

C   F   F#m7♭5   C

I have con - fi - dence in con - fi - dence a - lone; Be - sides which, you
I have con - fi - dence the world can all be mine. They'll have to a -

C°7   G7   **1.** C   Am

see, I have con - fi - dence in me. ___
gree I have con - fi - dence in

2. Dm7   G7   C   F   C

___ me. ___

The Lonely Goatherd

Lyrics by Oscar Hammerstein II
Music by Richard Rodgers

First note

Verse
Brightly

1. High on a hill was a lone-ly goat-herd, lay-ee o - dl, lay-ee o - dl lay-ee-o.
2. prince on the bridge of a cas-tle moat heard: lay-ee o - dl, lay-ee o - dl lay-ee-o.
3 One lit-tle girl in a pale pink coat heard: lay-ee o - dl, lay-ee o - dl lay-ee-o.

Loud was the voice of the lone-ly goat-herd, lay-ee o - dl, lay-ee o - dl - o.
Men on a road, with a load to tote, heard: lay-ee o - dl, lay-ee o - dl - o.
She yo-deled back to the lone-ly goat-herd, lay-ee o - dl, lay-ee o - dl - o.

Folks in a town that was quite re-mote heard: lay-ee o - dl, lay-ee o - dl lay-ee-o.
Men in the midst of a ta-ble d'hote heard: lay-ee o - dl, lay-ee o - dl lay-ee-o.
Soon her ma-ma with a gleam-ing gloat heard: lay-ee o - dl, lay-ee o - dl lay-ee-o.

Lust-y and clear from the goat-herd's throat heard: lay-ee o - dl, lay-ee o - dl - o.
Men drink-in' beer with the foam a-float heard: lay-ee o - dl, lay-ee o - dl - o.
What a du-et for a girl and a goat-herd, lay-ee o - dl, lay-ee o - dl - o.

Maria

Lyrics by Oscar Hammerstein II
Music by Richard Rodgers

How do you solve a prob - lem like Ma - ri - a?

How do you catch a cloud and pin it down?

How do you find a word that means Ma - ri - a? A

flib - ber - ti - gib - bet! A will - o' - the - wisp! A clown!

Man - y a thing you know you'd like to tell her;

Man - y a thing she ought to un - der - stand. But

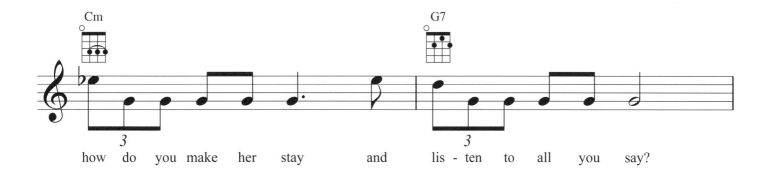

how do you make her stay and lis - ten to all you say?

How do you keep a wave up - on the sand? Oh,

how do you solve a prob - lem like Ma - ri - a?

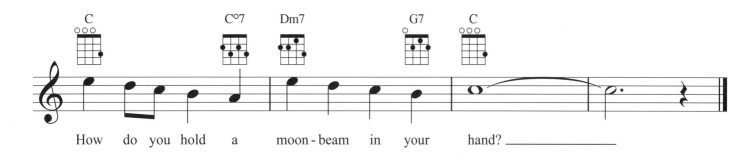

How do you hold a moon - beam in your hand? _____

My Favorite Things

Lyrics by Oscar Hammerstein II
Music by Richard Rodgers

these are a few of my fa - vor - ite

things.

fa - vor - ite things.

Verse

3. Girls in white dress - es with

blue sat - in sash - es, snow - flakes that

stay on my nose and eye - lash - es,

sil - ver white win - ters that melt in - to springs,

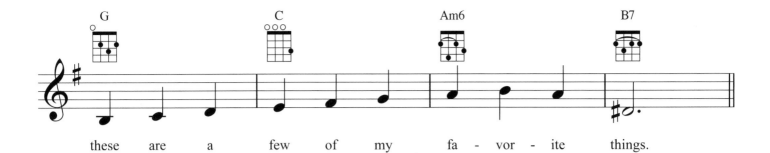

these are a few of my fa - vor - ite things.

Outro

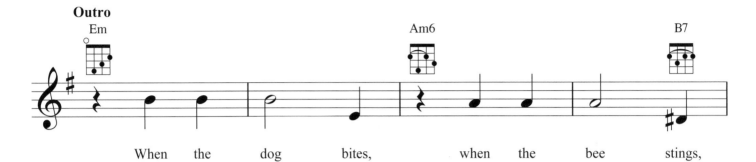

When the dog bites, when the bee stings,

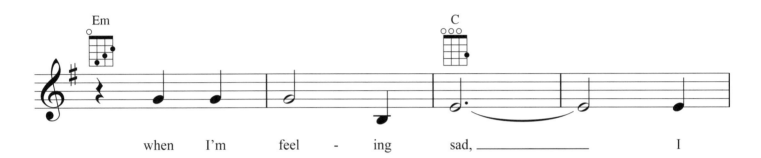

when I'm feel - ing sad, _____ I

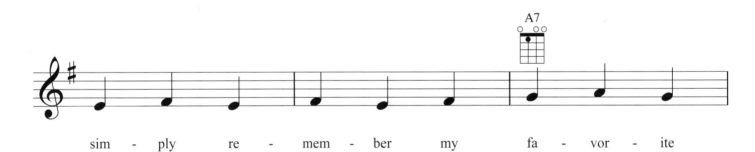

sim - ply re - mem - ber my fa - vor - ite

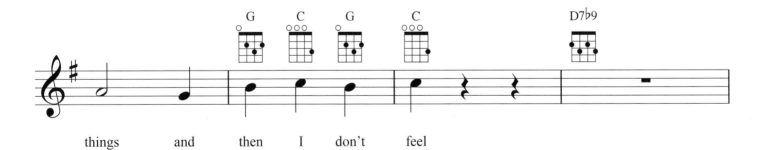

things and then I don't feel

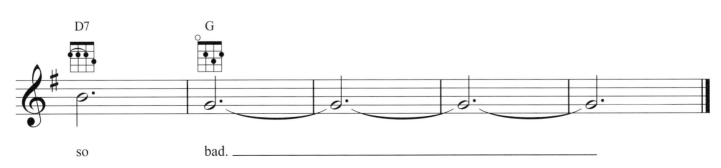

so bad. _____

Do-Re-Mi

Lyrics by Oscar Hammerstein II
Music by Richard Rodgers

Doe, a deer, a fe-male deer, Ray, a drop of gold-en sun, Me, a name I call my-self, Far, a long, long way to run. Sew, a nee-dle pull-ing thread, La, a note to fol-low sew, Tea, a drink with jam and bread, that will bring us back to do! Do-re-mi-fa-so-la-ti-do!

Sixteen Going On Seventeen

Lyrics by Oscar Hammerstein II
Music by Richard Rodgers

So Long, Farewell

Lyrics by Oscar Hammerstein II
Music by Richard Rodgers

1. So long, fare-well, Auf wie-der-sehn, good-night. __ I
(2.) long, fare-well, Auf wie-der-sehn, a-dieu. __ A-
(3.) long, fare-well, Au' voir, auf wie-der-sehn. __ I'd

hate to go and leave this pret-ty sight. __ *(Instrumental)*
dieu, a-dieu, to yieu and yieu and yieu. __
like to stay and taste my first cham-pagne. __

2., 3. So 4. So

long, fare-well, Auf wie-der-sehn, good-bye, __ I leave and heave a

sigh and say good-bye. __ Good-bye. __

Slower Cmaj7 · · · **Verse** C

5. I'm glad to go, I can - not tell a

lie. ___ I flit, I float, I fleet - ly flee, I fly. ___

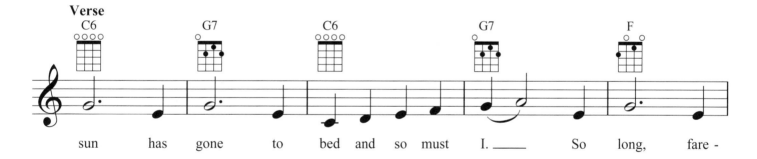

G7 · C6 · G7

(Instrumental) 6. The

Verse C6 · G7 · C6 · G7 · F

sun has gone to bed and so must I. ___ So long, fare -

C · F · C **Outro** D7

well, Auf wie - der - sehn, good - bye. ___ Good - bye, _____ Good-

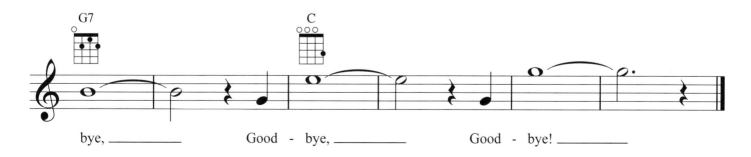

G7 · C

bye, _____ Good - bye, _____ Good - bye! _____

Something Good

Lyrics and Music by Richard Rodgers

The Sound of Music

Lyrics by Oscar Hammerstein II
Music by Richard Rodgers

Outro-Chorus

23

Wedding Processional

Lyrics by Oscar Hammerstein II
Music by Richard Rodgers

First note

Majestically

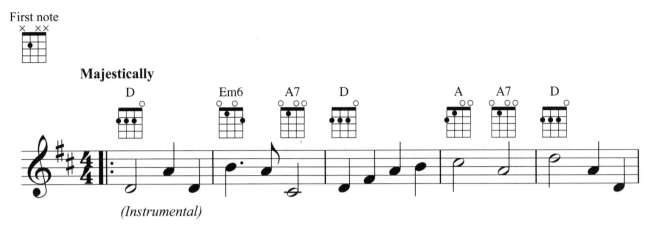

(Instrumental)

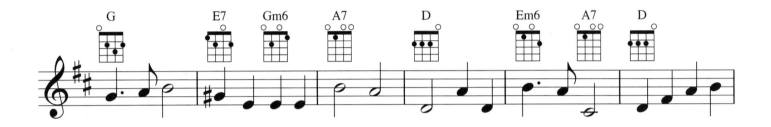

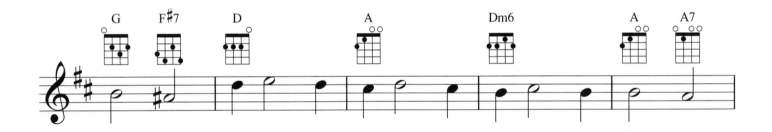

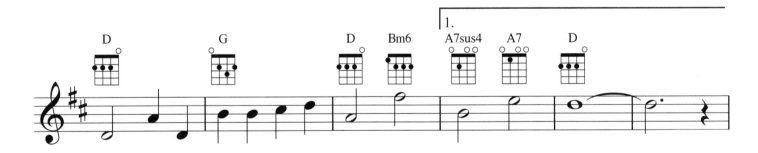

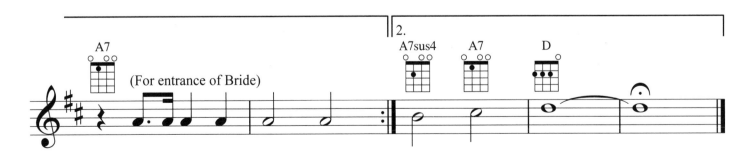

(For entrance of Bride)